EASTERN FRONT F

MW00454793

THE WAFFEN SS
IN THE EAST 1941-1943

NICHOLAS MILTON

Pen & Sword
MILITARY

This edition published in 2013 by
Pen & Sword Military
An imprint of
Pen & Sword Books Ltd
47 Church Street
Barnsley
South Yorkshire
S70 2AS

First published in Great Britain in 2011 in digital format by
Coda Books Ltd.

Copyright © Coda Books Ltd, 2011
Published under licence by Pen & Sword Books Ltd.

ISBN 978 1 78159 137 6

A CIP catalogue record for this book is
available from the British Library

Printed and bound in Great Britain by
CPI Group (UK) Ltd, Croydon, CR0 4YY

Pen & Sword Books Ltd incorporates the Imprints of Pen & Sword Aviation, Pen & Sword Family
History, Pen & Sword Maritime, Pen & Sword Military, Pen & Sword Discovery, Pen & Sword
Politics, Pen & Sword Atlas, Pen & Sword Archaeology, Wharncliffe Local History, Wharncliffe
True Crime, Wharncliffe Transport, Pen & Sword Select, Pen & Sword Military Classics, Leo
Cooper, The Praetorian Press, Claymore Press, Remember When, Seaforth Publishing and
Frontline Publishing

For a complete list of Pen & Sword titles please contact
PEN & SWORD BOOKS LIMITED
47 Church Street, Barnsley, South Yorkshire, S70 2AS, England
E-mail: enquiries@pen-and-sword.co.uk
Website: www.pen-and-sword.co.uk

FOREWORD

The *Waffen SS* combat record in the East has given them a deserved place as an elite fighting force in the history of the Second World War. However, the reputation of the *Waffen SS*, the armed political wing of the Schutzstaffel or Nazi party, will always be tainted by the war crimes they committed in the East including the killing of what the Nazi's termed untermenschen or sub humans – Slavs, Jews and Marxists. How did a small force designed to protect Adolf Hitler which numbered just 120 men in 1933 turn into one of the largest, most feared and efficient military machines the world has ever seen?

The answer lies in a speech Hitler gave to *Waffen SS* troops just three weeks before the start of Operation Barbarossa, the Nazi code name for the attack on the Soviet Union. He said "This is an ideological battle and a struggle of races. Here stands a world as we conceived it – beautiful, decent, socially equal and full of culture; this is what our Germany is like. On the other side stands a population of 180,000,000, a mixture of races, whose very names are unpronounceable and whose physique is such that one can only shoot them down without mercy or compassion. When you fight over there in the east, you are carrying on the same struggle against the same sub-humanity, the same inferior races, that at one time appeared under the name of Huns, another time of Magyars, another time of Tartars, and still another time under the name of Genghis Khan and the Mongols. Today they appear as Russians under the political banner of Bolshevism."

When he launched operation Barbarossa Hitler ordered the *Wehrmacht* or German Army to conquer the Soviet Union and the *Waffen SS* to Nazisfy it. It was the biggest invasion in the history of human conflict. On one side were over three million well trained, equipped and battle hardened German troops including the *Waffen SS* and half a million of their Axis allies. In total the Germans had 153 divisions including 21 Panzer and 14 motorised divisions containing over 3400 tanks and 3000 aircraft. On the other side was a Soviet army of over five million men in 180 divisions with over 10,000 tanks and 20,000 aircraft. However, while on paper the Soviets seemed more than a match for the Germans, in reality their troops were badly organised and ill equipped and many of their tanks and aircraft were obsolete. Perhaps most importantly the Soviet army had lost many of its best commanders due to Stalin's purges.

To the *Wehrmacht* Hitler ordered the job of "kicking in the front door so the whole rotten Russian edifice will come tumbling down". To the *Waffen SS* fell not just the job of combat but also waging a race war to create Hitler's long cherished dream of *lebensraum* or living space for the German people in the East, a theory first mooted in his 1926 political testimony, *Mein Kampf*. Barbarossa was therefore always more than just a military campaign, it was a battle of ideologies between National Socialism and Communism to establish a new world order in Europe.

During operations in the East the *Waffen SS* grew from just six divisions comprising 160,000 men at the start of Barbarossa to a huge force of 38 combat divisions comprising over 950,000 men by the end of the war. With their distinctive uniforms, strict Germanic racial requirements and under the command of Heinrich Himmler, one of the post powerful men in the Third Reich, the *Waffen SS* earned a fearsome reputation for fighting. As a consequence they attracted only the most committed recruits who were willing to fight and die for the cause.

In the East *Waffen SS* divisions were placed under the operational control of the *Oberkommando des Heeres* or the Supreme High Command of the Army although in practice they often acted independently. While initially numerically insignificant when compared to the *Wehrmacht* or the Germany Army, the *Waffen SS* soon brought to Barbarossa an ideological fanaticism out of all proportion to their numbers.

For the over stretched German Army, with its history steeped in the old Imperial and Prussian traditions of solidarity and soldiering, indulging in any activities like racial cleansing which did not progress their war aims was regarded as a waste of resources. For the *Waffen SS* the regular army lacked the ideological zeal and fighting spirit to beat an opponent who would often rather die than be captured. The result was a severely strained relationship between the two who often disagreed on tactics at a time when they should have been combining forces to fight the Russians.

This sense of racial and military superiority, encouraged by Himmler through better pay, food and equipment, was central to the *Waffen SS* philosophy. It was combined with a fanatical loyalty to Hilter, best expressed in their motto *"Meine Ehre heisst Treue"* or "My honour is loyalty". It meant that at the start of Barbarossa the divisions which

Heinrich Himmler, *Reichsführer* of the SS.

comprised the *Waffen SS*, the *Leibstandarte Adolf Hitler, Das Reich, Totenkopf, Polizei* and *Nord* were all recruited from the toughest and most ideological ethnic Germans. The exception was the *Wiking* division which was recruited from Scandinavian, Finish, Estonian, Dutch and Belgian volunteers but served under German officers.

The *Wehrmacht* launched its surprise attack on Russia at 3.15 am on 22nd June 1941, bombing positions in Soviet occupied Poland. Attached to the three huge army groups were the six *Waffen SS* divisions. Army Group North advanced through the Baltic States and on to Leningrad, accompanied by *Totenkopf* , *Polizei* and *Nord*. Army Group Centre headed towards Moscow with the *Das Reich*. *Leibstandarte* and *Wiking* were with Army Group South and marched towards the Ukraine and Kiev.

During the first six months of Barbarossa the sheer scale of the Soviet rout in the East surprised even the German generals. On the opening day alone the *Luftwaffe* destroyed over 2000 Soviet aircraft, many on the ground and Army Group North penetrated over 50 miles into Russian territory. By the end of the first week Army Group Centre had captured Minsk and by the end of June they had advanced over 200 miles towards Moscow. By the end of September Army Group South had captured nearly half a million Soviet troops during the Battle of Kiev and Army Group North had lay siege to Leningrad. At the spearhead of all these successful advances in the East was the *Waffen SS*.

Yet just three months later the offensive ground to a shuddering halt on 1 December 1941 in temperatures of minus 40 Fahrenheit on the outskirts of Moscow. Five days later the Red Army counter attacked driving the Germans back 40 miles. During Operation Typhoon or the attack on Moscow *Das Reich* suffered big losses and of the 2000 soldiers who had started out with the regiment that June only 35 were left alive by the end of December. While the defeat was a crushing defeat for Germany, it was to prove the making of the *Waffen SS*.

By the end of 1941 the *Waffen SS* had suffered over 43,000 casualties across the Eastern Front. One in four troops had either been killed or wounded. However, it was widely recognised even by the *Wehrmacht* that they had fought with great tenacity and without them the German army would not have got to the gates of Moscow. Eberhard von Macksensen, commander of III Army Corps in Army Group South, writing to Himmler said the *Leibstandarte* had demonstrated "inner discipline, cool daredevilry, cheerful enterprise, unshakeable firmness in a crisis, exemplary toughness and camaraderie". The legend of the fanatical fighting spirit of the *Waffen SS* had been born.

By the beginning of 1942 the Soviet Union was bloodied but unbowed. The changing fortunes of the campaign were shown by the encirclement of 100,000 Germans troops from Army Group North in the Demyansk pocket, south of Leningrad in February. They included the *SS Division Totenkopf* who again were at the forefront of the fighting and led the breakout in April. However, they paid a high price with 15,000 troops either killed or wounded. After this the *Waffen SS* were never again to regain the initiative in the East but were to fight with distinction at Stalingrad and later at Kharkov and Kursk.

Operation Barbarossa was to bestow many honours on *Waffen SS* soldiers for outstanding bravery included Jospeh "Sepp" Dietrich, Paul "Pappa" Hauser, Helmuth Becker, Max Simon, Christian Tyschen and Karl-Heinz Boska, all pictured in this book. Also shown is Gerardus Mooyman who as a Dutch national was the first non German to receive the Knights Cross of the Iron Cross, the highest honour that Germany could award a soldier for outstanding bravery.

When historians review the campaign in the East the fighting record of the *Waffen SS* is rightly seen in the context of Hitler's ideological war against the Soviet Union. As a result there is an indelible stain on their combat record and after the war many *Waffen SS* veterans were deprived of pension rights. While some were involved in atrocities, others fought honourably given the fog of war which afflicted both sides. As these pictures show many *Waffen SS* troops distinguished themselves in combat and showed incredible bravery, often against overwhelming odds.

Operation Barbarossa was the German codename for the attack on Russia. It commenced at 3.15 am on 22nd June 1941. Over 3 million German troops and half a million of its Axis allies attacked across an 1800 mile front in three massive army groups. The *Wehrmacht* or German army was accompanied by six *Waffen SS* Divisions.

Army Group North advanced through the Baltic States and on to Leningrad, accompanied by *Totenkopf, Polizei* and *Nord.* Army Group Centre headed towards Moscow with the *Das Reich. Leibstandarte* and *Wiking* were with Army Group South and travelled towards the Ukraine and Kiev.

A German motorcycle and side car struggle through the mud. The Germans suffered high losses in tanks and vehicles in the autumn rains which turned many roads into a quagmire.

Waffen SS troops rest during the opening months of the campaign.
Soldiers had to walk up to 40 miles a day to keep up with the Panzers.

A *Waffen SS* soldier with an MG 42 machine gun. Robust and reliable it fired over 1000 rounds a minute.

Motorcycles of the *Wiking Division* scout ahead of the Panzers. The speed and ferocity of the German attack caught the Russians completely by surprise.

A close up of a *Totenkopf* motorcycle. Note the swastika on the side car, used for recognition by the *Luftwaffe*.

German vehicles speed along a road during the initial phase of Operation Barbarossa. Later in the campaign roads were to become all but impassable due to rain then snow.

Crossing the River Beresina Soviet partisans blow up a bridge, destroying a German assault gun. The *Waffen SS* unit survived the 8 metre drop.

A knocked out Russian T34 tank. The mainstay of the Soviet army it was more than equal to the German Panzers at the beginning of the campaign and was only later outclassed by the German Panzer VI (Tiger) and Panther.

German soldiers dig in at Borodino, Russia. The vast distances involved across the 1800 mile front posed huge logistical problems to both the *Wehrmacht* and the *Waffen SS*.

A shot down Russian Rata aircraft. In the opening days of the campaign much of the Soviet airforce was destroyed on the ground before it could take off, with over 2000 planes destroyed on the first day alone.

Destroyed Russian anti tank guns and lorry's litter the side of the road. Many forward Russian positions were bombed by the *Luftwaffe* and then abandoned by the retreating Soviet troops.

A *Waffen SS Das Reich* unit give the Hitler salute and a salvo is fired in honour of a dead *Kameraden* or comrade, killed during the first days of the campaign.

The burial of members of the *1st SS Motorcycle Battalion*, killed in fighting with Soviet troops near Yelnia. General of the Panzer Troops, Heinrich von Vietinghoff -Scheel, said *"We stand in respect and awe at such heroism"*.

Later in the campaign as German military losses mounted, soldiers were quickly buried where they fell and the grave marked by a helmet on a rifle.

Oberführer Bittrich, commander of the *2nd SS Panzer division Das Reich*, enjoys a cigarette with a soldier outside his regimental HQ in the summer of 1941.

Members of the reconnaissance *Battalion Das Reich Division* are awarded the Iron Cross for bravery during the opening months of the campaign, 25 July 1941.

An SS grenadier proudly displays his, *Eisernes Kreuz 2 Klasse* or Iron Cross 2nd Class for bravery on the battlefield, 1941. Over four and a half million Iron Crosses were awarded in World War Two.

Waffen SS troops storm a village during Operation Barbarossa. The Germans were surprised that the Soviets vigorously defended even quite small villages.

A 7.5cm *leichtes Infanteriegeschütz* 18 or 7.5cm le.IG 18, infantry support gun is brought up to support the troops. It had a rate of fire of 8 -12 rounds per minute and a range of 3550 metres. The crew put their fingers in their ears to reduce the noise.

An *SS Totenkopf Panzerabwehrkanone* 36 or 3.7cm anti tank gun is towed towards the front, 1941. A lightweight gun, it was of little use against the Russian T34 tanks so acquired the derisory nickname *Heeresanklopfgerät*, or *"tank door knocker"*. It was replaced a year later by the more powerful 5cm Pak 38.

Soldiers advance behind two *Waffen SS Das Reich Sonderkraftfahrzeug 251* or Sd.Kfz251 halftracks. It was the largest and best armoured German halftrack and was designed to take the *Panzergrenadiers* or the motorised infantry into battle.

This Sd.Kfz251 halftrack has been blown up by a Russian mine. The retreating Soviets mined roads, fields and villages, slowing the German advance.

A 20mm Flak 30 anti aircraft gun is brought up to support the attack. Although designed as an anti aircraft gun it was also extensively used as an infantry support gun. It was the most numerous German artillery gun produced during the war.

The village of Mashina near Yuchnow burns on 7 October 1941. The Germans would often find either stiff resistance or deserted villages which were heavily mined. Either way they would take their revenge by setting light to them.

The *6th Panzer Division Das Nord* fought with Army Group North and saw action right up to the Arctic Circle. Here they have brought up a *7.5cm leichtes Infanteriegeschütz* 18 or 7.5cm le.IG 18 infantry support gun to fire on partisans hiding in the woods and marshes of Karelia.

Waffen SS soldiers take cover behind the shield of a 7.5cm le.IG 18 infantry support gun.

Totenkopf troops leave behind a Russian burning village in the opening weeks of Barbarossa, 21st June 1941. The division was notorious for its ethnic cleansing. It's Deaths Head insignia reflected the fact that many early recruits were concentration camp guards.

SS Cavalry Division troops cross a swollen river during Barbarossa. When the autumn rains came even small fords could become impassable, resulting in troops often having to travel miles out of their way to find a safe place to cross.

Das Reich troops in a Russian village during the opening weeks of the campaign, June 1941. They were attached to Army Group centre whose objective was to take Moscow. Note the *Wolfsangel* or Wolf's Hook insignia on the front right wheel arch, the symbol for *Das Reich*.

Totenkopf troops rest in a copse during a lull in the fighting, September 1941. They were attached to Army Group North who advanced through the Baltic States and on to Leningrad.

Totenkopf troops crossing a makeshift bridge in a Horsh 108 troop carrier. Note the Deaths Head insignia on the rear.

The Reconnaissance Battlion of the *SS Wiking Division* scout ahead of the infantry and tanks. *Wiking Division* was recruited from Scandinavian, Finish, Estonian, Dutch and Belgian volunteers but served under German officers.

Waffen SS troops using an anti tank gun against the Soviet T34 tank. The T34 was heavily armoured and it required a direct hit to its tracks or at very close range to disable it.

Sepp Dietrich, commander *Leibstandarte*, watches over the advance of his troops. He was one of Nazi Germany's most decorated soldiers.

SS Totenkopf officers drive to the front in a Volkswagen Kubeklwagen Type 82, the German equivalent of a jeep, 1941. Although more comfortable than a jeep, its low centre of gravity meant it struggled with the deep mud in Russia.

Paul "Papa" Hauser, lieutenant-general of the *2nd SS Division Das Reich*, receives the Knights Cross of the Iron Cross from General of the Panzer Troops, Heinrich von Vietinghoff-Scheel. He was highly respected by his troops and known as the *"father"* of the *Waffen SS*.

A *Waffen SS* officer and *Wehrmacht* troops listen to a briefing at the Russian Front. The *Wehrmacht* and the *Waffen SS* had a strained relationship during the open stages of Barbarossa.

Supplies are brought to the front by horses at dusk. Infantry and horse drawn artillery still formed the bulk of the three German army groups attacking Russia. There were 750,000 horses in the German army at the start of Barbarossa.

A *Waffen SS* soldier from *Leibstandarte Division* watches a village burn. As the campaign progressed many Soviet fighters rather than surrender went into the hiding and formed partisan units who operated behind German lines.

A salvo is fired into the air to honour a German soldier killed in action. Operation Barbarossa accounted for 95% of German casualties between 1941 and 1944.

In Germany a march past of the *Leibstandarte* on *Heldengedenktag* or Heroes Day. It was previously known as *Volkstrauetag* or Commemoration Day, a national day of mourning for all those who had been killed in battle but the Nazis turned into a day to celebrate the heroism, not the sacrifice of German troops.

Leibstandarte troops fight on the outskirts of the port of Mariupol in Ukraine. The city fell on 8 October 1941 giving the Germans access to the Sea of Azov.

Mariupol burns. The Germans were to lose control of the city two years
later as they retreated from the advancing Soviet army.

Panzers attack Soviet forces still holding out in Mariupol. The attack on Russia would see German and Axis troops attacking in three huge army groups along a vast front which grew longer as they advanced.

A *Waffen SS Leinstandarte* BMW R75 motorcyclist and his outrider watch as buildings burn. The German army insisted that both BMW and their rivals Zündapp use almost 70% of the same motorcycle components to simplify the supply of spares.

Waffen SS Funker or radio operator receives a message for his unit. The attack on Russia posed a serious challenge in terms of communication because of the speed of the advance and the great distances involved along the fronts.

An SS radio operator receives their next orders. Good communication between the Panzer tanks and the infantry following them ensured that in the opening months of Barbarossa the Germans retained tactical surprise.

Waffen SS troops on patrol. They were feared by the Soviets due to the fanaticism they brought to the fighting.

Das Reich troops cross a river after the Soviets had blown up the bridge. The Germans attack depended upon Panzer engineers being able to quickly establish temporary pontoon bridges capable of supporting tanks.

A German dug out on the Eastern Front in 1941. Morale among troops in the early months of the campaign was very high and most of the German high command thought that the campaign would be over by Christmas.

Waffen SS troops firing an MG 42 machine gun. It was the standard machine gun from 1942 onwards replacing the M34 and had one of the highest rates of fire of any single barrelled gun at 1200 – 1500 rounds per minute.

Waffen SS troops man a machine gun post covering the approach road to Louhi, 1941. In 1941 the German advance was so swift that they would encircle Russian armies who would then become trapped miles behind the front line.

By late 1941 the Russian winter, ferocity of the fighting and the large distances involved in Barbarossa were beginning to affect morale among the German troops who released that they were in for a long battle of attrition.

German soldiers sort out ammunition for their unit. The sheer speed of the advance during the early months of Barbarossa meant that providing enough ammunition for the troops was a constant logistical challenge.

A German troop reflects on the battle during a lull in the fighting. Their hopes that Barbarossa would all be over by Christmas was shattered by the stall in the advance of Army Group Centre outside the gates of Moscow in December 1941.

General Sillasvuo was the Commander of the III Finish Army which included the *Waffen SS Nord Division*. The Fins enthusiastically joined in the attack on Russia to get their revenge for the Winter War of 1939-40. This saw the Red Army humiliated but through sheer numbers overrun the country.

In 1941 Finland committed 16 divisions and 3 Brigades, consisting of 475 000 men and women to Operation Barbarossa.

SS officers relax during the opening weeks of operation Barbarossa. Despite their quick advance, officers had noticed a difference in the campaign compared to the West with many more Soviet troops prepared to fight and die rather than surrender.

Soldiers from the *Wiking Division* use a flamethrower against Soviet troops. This Model 35 flamethrower had a capacity of 2.5 gallons and a range of 25 yards. They were operated by engineers rather than combat troops and were most effective at close range against pillboxes.

To the annoyance of German Generals, Finland while keen to recover the ground lost to the Russians in the Winter War, would not push further into the Soviet Union.

The *SS Calvalry Brigade* in 1941. It was mainly involved in anti partisan operations. In 1942 it was upgraded into *8th SS Cavalry Division* or *Florian Geyer*.

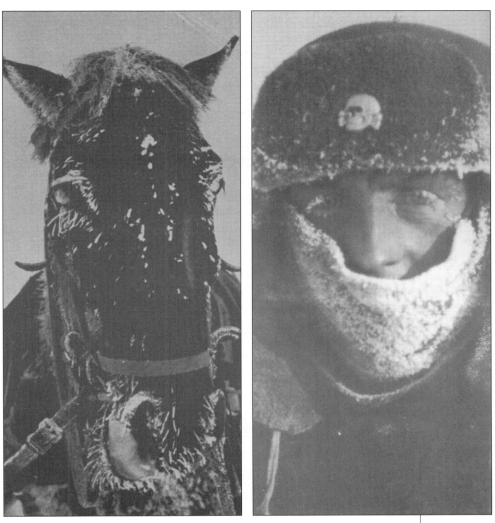

During the Russian winter of 1941 temperatures of minus 20 degrees Fahrenheit were common affecting both men and animals.

The Russian winter of 1941 came early and by November it had begun to seriously affect the morale of German troops. The Soviet counteroffensives launched in December further exhausted and demoralized the German troops.

The Russian winter took a very heavy toll on the Germans who unlike the Soviets were not equipped with winter clothing. By November 1941, the Germans had suffered an unprecedented 730,000 casualties.

The spring thaw of 1942 when it finally came turned many roads into a quagmire. The mud and later the snow caused repeated delays in the advance and highlighted the lack of proper logistical planning for the campaign.

Infantry troops trudge past a Panzer during the Russian winter. The Panzers with their complex engineering were not suited to the freezing Soviet winter unlike the Russian T34 tanks which being a much simpler design were easier to repair.

Waffen SS troops were considered an elite and received the best equipment and clothing. But in the winter of 1941 they still lacked the winter uniforms needed to fight effectively in the Russian winter.

A *Waffen SS Oberscharführer* or platoon leader scans the horizon for Soviet troops. The Russian winter gave the Soviets a respite from the German advance and allowed them to plan their counter offensive.

During the Russian winter of 1941 German troops soon became experts at putting up makeshift shelters against the cold.

The harsh Russian winter caused chaos with German transport and lines of communication. In sub zero temperatures fires had to be lit under the engines of lorry's and other vehicles to help them start.

Waffen SS troops with an MG34 heavy machine gun. The legs could be extended to allow it to be used as an anti-aircraft gun or lowered so it could be used as an infantry support weapon.

An *SS Calvary Division* patrol during the winter of 1941. The deep snow slowed the German advance in November and played a key role in the halting the German offensive in December.

White winter overcoats were issued to advancing German troops but underneath many still had summer clothing. As a result frostbite took a terrible toll and many troops lost limbs or were deemed unfit to fight.

Troops are relieved at the front line. German soldiers were given three weeks leave but due to problems with transport and the great distances involved in getting back to Germany often only spent a week with their families.

Waffen SS troops had to improvise during the Russian winter, resorting to horses and sledges to transfer equipment to the front. They also supplemented their uniforms with Russian clothing to keep warm regardless of the strict dress regulations.

A gun tractor with a light field howitzer gets stuck in a snow drift. The Germans often had to resort to horses to pull their equipment out of deep snow as animals proved much more suited to the freezing temperatures.

Waffen SS troops put together a "Panzer cocktail", an improvised Molotov cocktail used against the Russian T34 tank. Due to its sloping armour the Germans 3.7cm anti tank gun proved ineffective against it.

German troops shovel snow to keep their lines of communication open. It often proved a futile task and during the winter of 1941 some units were cut off for weeks.

The Russian winter of 1941/1942 was the hardest in 120 years with a record temperature of over minus 40 degrees Fahrenheit recorded in December. Unlike the Russians the Germans were not trained or equipped to fight in such conditions.

German troops build an igloo as a defensive shield around a mortar. Blocks of ice proved to be very good at deflecting and absorbing enemy fire.

During January 1942 many German soldiers found survival let along fighting difficult in the Russian winter.

A soldier takes over a position following the encirclement of German troops in the Demyansk pocket south of Stalingrad, February 1942.

German soldiers try to pull a lorry out of the snow. The sub zero temperatures which often reached minus 20 degrees Fahrenheit and deep snow suited the Russians who were used to such conditions and were fighting on home territory.

Trapped in the Demyansk pocket was the *SS Totenkopf Division*, part of 100,000 men surrounded by the Soviets.

The *4th SS Polizei Division* advances on Leningrad. The siege of Leningrad started on 8th September 1941 and was not lifted until 27 January 1944. At 372 days long it was one of the longest and most costly sieges in history.

In the middle of February the weather improved enough to allow the *Luftwaffe* to resupply the trapped German troops. A breakout in April lead by the T*otenkopf Division* cost nearly 15,000 men killed or wounded.

Das Reich, part of Army Group Centre, reached the gates of Moscow in December 1941 but the weather, massive losses and a Soviet counteroffensive forced the division back.

Waffen SS snipers on the Eastern Front. He is equipped with the standard German army rifle the Karbiner 98k Kurz with a telescopic sight. Rifles which were exceptionally accurate in factory tests were specifically allocated to snipers for this task. They had an effective range of 1000 metres.

Snipers generally worked in pairs, one scanning the horizon looking for targets, the other taking the shots.

German troops form defensive positions on the River Moskva near Moscow, 3 December 1941. Two days later Operation Typhoon or the German attack on Moscow was repelled when 18 Soviet Siberian divisions specialising in winter warfare joined the Russian army.

From their positions west of Moscow soldiers in *Das Reich* could clearly see the Soviet capital through their binoculars. It was the closet they would ever get. The German army would never again threaten the Russian capital.

Soldiers from *Das Reich Division* rest on the outskirts of Moscow, December 1941. The division was decimated by the Soviet counter offensive and was withdrawn for rest and refitting.

A Finnish volunteer battalion III, part of the *6th Waffen SS Nord Division*, battles its way through a snow storm. Most of the Finnish army refused to invade the Soviet Union but were remobilised in 1944 when the Russian advance again threatened their country.

The *Waffen SS* use high explosives and mines to blow up dams of ice blocking a river.

The Germans also used mines against the Soviet T34 tank. With its thick sloping armour the Germans found the Russian tank a formidable opponent.

A 3.7cm anti-tank gun is towed along on runners by horses. The gun while an effective infantry support weapon proved ineffective against Russian tanks like the T34 and KV 1 and 2.

A German soldier loads a magazine for his K98 rifle. Although comparable to Soviet weapons at the beginning of the campaign, its slow rate of fire became a handicap when the Russians began to be equipped with semi-automatic weapons.

A German convoy makes slow progress through a snow storm. The Russian weather demoralised the German troops as did their distance from home. Nearly a thousand miles separated Moscow and Berlin.

German troops take cover in a copse and scan the horizon. In the depths of winter woods not only provided cover from the enemy but also as importantly from the elements.

Red army soldiers surrender during the winter of 1941. In the first weeks of Operation Typhoon or the Battle of Moscow hundreds of thousands of Soviets were taken prisoner.

Gerardus Mooyman, a Dutch national and a soldier with the *4th SS Volunteer Panzergrenadier Brigade Netherland*s was awarded the Knights Cross of the Iron Cross for knocking out 13 Soviet tanks in one day during battle at Lake Ladoga. He was the first non German to receive the award.

A *Waffen SS* soldier emerges from his dug out. Over 100,000 German troops suffered from frostbite, the more serious cases requiring amputation.

German troops do exercises and try to keep warm during the Russian winter. They lacked proper winter clothing and their great coats despite being made of wool offered little in the way of insulation. In contrast the Soviets wore quilted coats.

Waffen SS troops collapse exhausted after fierce fighting. As well as the winter, tiredness and hunger took their toll on the Germans fighting spirit.

German troops pose behind the machine gun field on a Sdkfz 251 halftrack. As well as transporting troops they were used to tow anti tank and field artillery guns.

A *Waffen SS* tank crew emerges from a Panzer. The Panzer III was the German tank most used in the opening stages of Operation Barbarossa but it was outclassed in every respect by the Soviet T34.

An abandoned *Wiking* motorcycle and sidecar. The spring and autumn rains in Russia were known as the "mud season" and they claimed many valuable vehicles severely hampering the German war effort.

Waffen SS engineers, one in their distinctive camouflage uniform, help to build a road. Although making sure that roads were passable was the job of engineers, in practice it was a preoccupation of all soldiers because it was such a mammoth task.

Army Group South with the *SS Leibstandarte* and *Wiking Divisions* marched through the Ukraine and towards the valuable Caucasus oilfields. There they ran into fierce resistance but made better progress after being reinforced by Army Group Centre. Despite this the rains still made progress difficult.

In operation Barbarossa horses proved to be much more reliable than the mechanised might of the *Waffen SS*. The German Army had over 750,000 horses at the start of the campaign in contrast to only about 600,000 motor vehicles, including some 3,500 armoured fighting vehicles.

A lorry abandoned to the floods in the Demyansk pocket, early 1942. The trapped troops were provided with 266 tonnes of supplies from the air each day by the *Luftwaffe*.

Russian peasants watch as a German motorcycle and side car rushes past towards the front. As untermenschen or sub humans the Germans treated them with contempt which simply stiffened their resolve to fight.

An *SS Totenkopf Cavalry* bands plays marching songs, 1942. In Russia when the bad weather set in during the autumn and the roads turned into a quagmire, cavalry troops were often best suited to pushing ahead. They also played a vital role in maintaining morale.

The *8th SS Calvary Division* was named after Florian Geyer, a sixteenth century nobleman who was famous for leading the peasants during the German Peasants War.

A lone sentry stands guard on Hill 252 near Zdenac. German forces were frequently subjected to attack by Russian partisans who operated with great bravery behind enemy lines.

The German Army lost an average of 1,000 horses a day during Barbarossa. About three quarters of these losses were due to combat, the rest due to heart failure brought on by overwork disease, exposure, and starvation.

Blacksmiths shoe a horse. At the start of the war the Germans only had one cavalry division but due to the nature of the fighting on the Russian front they finished the war with seven, all mostly in the *Waffen SS*.

To feed three horses doing useful work such as pulling guns and equipment required the services of two more horses to haul their weekly rations of feed and fodder.

The Germans made extensive use of horses throughout the war, here carrying food in thermos containers. During Barbarossa they lost about 2.7 million animals, nearly double the 1.4 million that were lost in World War One.

Waffen SS engineers build a bridge while others bathe naked in the river. Engineers were attached to every unit and were a vital part of the German war effort, helping to overcome whatever obstacles were placed in the way of the advancing army.

A *Waffen SS* Cavalry brigade. As well as the *SS Division Florian Geyer Division*, mounted infantry regiments were operating as autonomous units with the army during 1942 and 1943.

Waffen SS soldiers attached to Army Group South cross the River Pripyat in the Ukraine. They were surrounded by vast marshes which provided many hiding places for Soviet partisans who regularly attacked the German advance.

Unlike abandoned vehicles, dead or lame horses were of value even when they could no longer be used for combat purposes. As a result they were often killed for food by Germans and Russians alike.

A German motorcyclist sunbathes. Motorcyclists were crucial to the German offensive being more mobile and able to cover large distances much more quickly than other motorised vehicles.

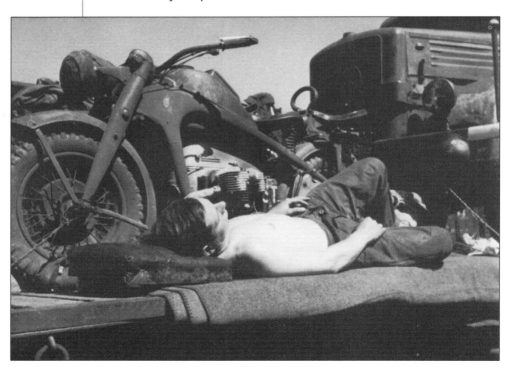

A Panzer III tank rolls forward towards the front line. Outclassed by the Russian T34 and KV tanks and difficult to repair, the Panzer III was nevertheless the core of the German mechanised divisions and over 5700 were built.

SS Wiking Division soldiers hitch a lift on a Panzer III tank, 1942. Due to continuing losses at the hands of the Russian T34 tank a year later the Panzer III was superseded by the Panzer IV and the Panther.

Waffen SS troops in Yugoslavia. It was overrun by Germans forces just before the start of Operation Barbarossa in what became known as the April War and *Waffen SS* units continued to operate there throughout the campaign in the East.

Invading Yugoslavia delayed the onset of the attack on Russia. Throughout operation Barbarossa partisans kept valuable *Waffen SS* units pinned down and away from the Eastern Front.

General Model talks with his Ia or general staff officer *Standartenfüehrer* Ostendorf at the command headquarters of *Das Reich*. Model was a brilliant tactician who successfully defended the front of Army Group Centre throughout 1942 and 1943.

Felix Steiner, commander of the *SS Wiking Division*. Chosen by *SS Reichsführer* Heinrich Himmler to lead the Division, Steiner created an elite and highly motivated fighting force from Scandinavian, Finish, Estonian, Dutch and Belgian volunteers.

An SS radio operator receives their next orders. Good communication between the Panzer tanks and the infantry was what made the German war machine so successful.

A *Waffen SS* radio operator climbs on a roof to erect an aerial. Radio and reconnaissance units were particularly targeted by Soviet partisans to disrupt German lines of communication which were already stretched by the vast distances involved in the campaign.

The insignia of the *Wiking, Totenkopf, Leibstandarte* and *Das Reich SS Divisions*. Different symbols were used to identify each division and were prominently displayed with great pride.

A *Waffen SS* unit on operations against Soviet partisans. They were a resistance movement modelled on the Red Army who fought a guerrilla campaign against the Germans rear lines, successfully disrupting road and rail communications.

An *8cm Granatwerfer 34* mortar is carried through the woods. The barrel, baseplate, stand and shells all had to be carried by hand, making it a three man job to transport the mortar.

An *SS* officer talks with *Wehrmacht* commanders during Barbarossa. The *Waffen SS* and the *Wehrmacht* had a difficult relationship and often did not agree on strategy, meaning attacks were not always well co-ordinated.

A German soldier guards Russian prisoners. After 1941 the capture of large numbers of Soviet troops became much rarer with many preferring to fight and die rather than surrender.

Despite German propaganda stating that prisoners were treated in accordance with their rights as soldiers many Soviet prisoners were treated barbarically, especially by the *Waffen SS* in stark contradiction to the Geneva convention.

Soviet prisoners of war were treated in accordance with their supposed 'subhuman' Slavic racial status by the Germans. Of the 5.7 million Soviet prisoners taken by the German and their allies, over 3 million died in captivity.

Waffen SS troops scan the skyline from an armoured car. Armoured cars were used for reconnaissance and intelligence gathering, scouting ahead of mechanized units to assess enemy strength and location. Their primary role was to observe rather than fight enemy units, although they were expected to fight if engaged by the Soviets.

The German Army used several million bicycles during the Second
World War but they were better suited to the good roads in western
Europe than the rough tracks in Russia.

An *SS* reconnaissance patrol in action. Targeted by enemy soldiers at the front and partisans in the rear, they often suffered disproportionately high casualties.

A German *Panzerabwehrkanone* 7.5cm anti tank gun with 22 rings or hits to its credit. This versatile gun with a range of over 700 metres was the backbone of German anti tank artillery during Operation Barbarossa but it was heavy and often got bogged down in the mud.

A Soviet prisoner with a cigarette offers another a light watched by guards in a German propaganda photograph. News of the barbaric treatment of Soviet prisoners of war, who the *Waffen SS* claimed had not signed the Geneva convention, soon spread among the Soviet army.

The *7th SS Volunteer Mountain Division Prinz Eugen.* was formed in March 1942 from ethnic Germans volunteers from Vojvodina, Croatia, Hungary and Romania and was engaged in anti-partisan operations in the Balkans.

Hellmuth Becker, centre, later commander of the *3rd SS Panzer Division Totenkopf,* lies wounded in a trench after fierce fighting in the Demyansk pocket. He was awarded the Knights Cross of the Iron Cross for his bravery.

Waffen SS troops on their way to the Balkans. Partisan activity in the Balkans pinned down many *Waffen SS* units and kept them from reinforcing their comrades on the Eastern Front.

Max Simon, commander of the *1st Regiment of the Totenkopf Division*, was awarded the Knight's Cross for the fighting in the Battles of the Demyansk Pocket and promoted to *Oberführer* or Brigadier General. In December 1942 Simon was promoted again to *Brigadeführer* or Major General, prior to being given command of the *16th SS Panzergrenadier Division Reichsführer-SS*.

A *Waffen SS* anti aircraft gun protects a bridge being built by *Waffen SS* engineers. Although thousands of Soviet planes were destroyed during the opening months of Barbarossa, the Soviet air force regained the initiative in 1942 and became a much greater threat to the attacking Germans.

Soviet Partisans use a horn to call for the surrender of trapped German troops. Propaganda was an important tool for both sides during the campaign and the Germans and Russians made extensive use of leaflets dropped behind enemy lines.

A *Flak 30* or 20mm anti-aircraft gun in action. A lightweight gun it was easy to transport but its low fire power of only 120 rounds a minute let it down.

A *Panzerabwehrkanone 36* or 3.7cm gun protects a bridge, 1941. Bridges were prime targets for both the Soviet airforce and partisans.

Waffen SS troops had to contend with a wide variety of different conditions while fighting in Russia from the spring and autumn rains which would turn the ground into a quagmire to extreme heat in the summer.

Waffen SS troops cross a river on the Atlantic coast in August 1942. *Waffen SS* Divisions were withdrawn from the fierce fighting on the Eastern Front to rest, recuperate and be refitted in the West.

The *Leibstandarte* fought alongside *Das Reich* under the command of Paul "Papa" Hausser, third right, who was known as the father of the *Waffen SS*. For his services in Russia he was awarded the Knights Cross of the Iron Cross and Oak Leaves.

The *Feldpost* or field post with news from home was greatly looked forward to by the front line troops. It was subject to heavy censorship, particularly during the retreat from Russia in the latter years of the war.

A *Leibstandarte Schwerer Panzerspähwagen* or heavy armoured reconnaissance vehicle patrols the streets of a Russian town. This model was easy to spot because of the heavy "bedstead" antenna over the body of the vehicle used for the short wave radio.

Men of the *Wiking* division just prior to their attack on the vital city of Grozny in September 1942. During the battle the division was to lose over 1500 men and failed to capture the city. It was to be a turning point in its campaign and the first of many setbacks.

Waffen SS troops march up a slope following the crossing of a river somewhere in the Ukraine. Extensive use of pontoon boats was made for transferring men and equipment across water.

The German army also made regular use of inflatable boats or dinghys during operation Barbarossa. While they were capable of transporting men quickly across water, they were particularly vulnerable to enemy attack.

Waffen SS men relax prior to battle. They wore a wide range of uniforms from the *feldgrau* or field grey similar to the regular army to the mottled camouflage which was their hallmark.

A *Waffen SS* soldier shows the fatigue of battle. They earned a fearsome reputation for fighting and consequently were often the first choice of many young recruits over the other military services.

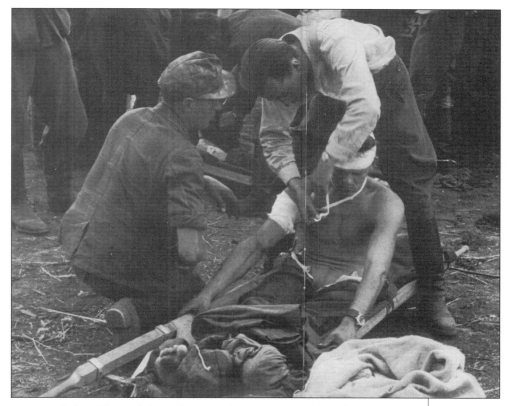

A wounded soldier of the *8th SS Calvary Division the Florian Geyer* receives help from the units doctor. The *Waffen SS* were feared and loathed in equal measure by the Russians for their fanatical fighting spirit and consequently suffered high casualties.

Waffen SS troops pull a motorcycle through the mud. Unlike in the West many Russian roads were not surfaced and quickly turned to mud after the rains.

Lorries make their way gingerly through a swollen river after the big thaw following the Soviet winter of 1941/42. The thaw could turn even a ford into a raging torrent.

A Panther tank makes its way upstream. Tanks coped better with the adverse conditions than many other types of armoured military vehicle but often proved difficult to repair when they did break down.

Waffen SS troops got better food and more rations than *Wehrmacht* troops which further strained the relationship.

Napoleons quote that an army marches on its stomach was especially true on the Eastern Front and the more generous rations which the *Waffen SS* received were vital in maintaining morale.

Waffen SS troops sort through the *fedlpost* or field post. The *Waffen SS* had their own post and officers made sure that the post got through to the front line whatever the conditions, mindful of how important it was to morale.

Waffen SS troops build a fire. Essential for keeping warm and cooking, they were also the only way to thaw engines frozen solid by the Russian winter.

A long line of rail wagons head back to Germany or the occupied territories. German lines of supply were stretched to the limit in Operation Barbarossa, tanks often having to be transported nearly a thousand miles.

The steady stream of supplies from Germany and the occupied territories was constantly under attack from Soviet partisans and aircraft. Partisans were parachuted in behind enemy lines and units formed in rural areas from peasants fleeing the German advance.

Soviet partisans blow up a railway track. Volunteers were recruited from the Red army and dropped behind the German lines. It was dangerous work. Any captured Soviet partisans were shot immediately.

An anti aircraft gun mounted on a railway wagon. The Soviet airforce found the long supply lines needed to maintain the German advance an easy target.

Supplies arrive at a German depot to be redistributed to the front line. As well as enemy attack the Germans had to contend with the fact that the railways in the Soviet Union were a wider gauge than in the West.

A *Waffen SS* communications outpost. Frequently the subject of partisan attacks, the Germans were also completely unaware that many of their secret messages were being read by the code breakers at Bletchley Park in Oxfordshire who in turn passed them on the Russians.

Waffen SS soldiers march towards the front. As the campaign turned against Germany morale in the *Wehrmacht* began to rapidly decline. In contrast the *Waffen SS* continued to fight fanatically.

Waffen SS troops advance cautiously in an armed vehicle. Soviet troops had learnt from the opening months of the campaign when they had often been caught and destroyed out in the open. Consequently they became experts at using the terrain to ambush German patrols.

A German Panzer 111 tank crew rest and watch the units mascot, a German Alsation dog. German officers were allowed to keep dogs which were not meant to be pets but working dogs designed to boost morale.

A Tiger tank commander with the *3rd SS Divison Totenkopf*. The division suffered heavy casualties during the Battle of the Demjansk Pocket but went on to fight with distinction at the Battle of Kursk in 1943.

Horses and tanks both played a pivotal role in Operation Barbarossa. While the Panzer tanks were mechanically complex and prone to breakdown, many horses were simply worked until they dropped from exhaustion, hunger or disease.

A Panzer III tank and a halftrack move across the Russian steppes in early 1942. The German offensive in the summer of 1942, called Case Blue, targeted the oil fields of Baku. Like 1941, the Germans again conquering vast amounts of territory but failed to achieve their military goals with the defeat at Stalingrad.

A *Waffen SS* motorcyclist stops to get his bearings, June 1942. Motorcyclists were crucial to the German offensive being more mobile and able to cover large distances much more quickly than other motorised vehicles.

Waffen SS troops inspect an unexploded rocket. The Soviet Katyusha rocket launcher took a heavy toll of both German troops and equipment. Compared to other artillery, multiple rocket launchers could deliver a devastating amount of explosives to a target area quickly. However, they had lower accuracy and required a longer time to reload than conventional artillery.

A wounded soldier from the *4th SS Division Polizei*. The division was officially formed in 1942 from its origins as a German police organisation. They took part in heavy fighting between January and March which resulted in the destruction of the Soviet 2nd Shock Army.

Waffen SS forces advance as part of Operation Blue in 1942. Overstretched by the vast area they had overrun, Germany forces would go on to fight an epic battle at Stalingrad which resulted in the destruction of the Sixth Army.

Exhausted and demoralised *Waffen SS* troops ride on a *Sonderkraftfahrzeug* or Sd.Kfz10, a special motorised vehicle, late 1942. The autumn rains again slowed the advance, putting great strain on both men and machines.

Waffen SS soldiers line up before a captured Russian T34 tank. The T34 inflicted huge losses on the attacking Germans due to its firepower, armour, speed and reliability.

The Germans were quick to utilise captured T34 tanks, marking them with German insignia. When introduced in 1940 it was the most advanced tank design in the world. Although by 1943 outclassed by other tanks such as the German Panther, it remained a formidable opponent.

Waffen SS enginners carry out vital repairs to a Sd.Kfz251 halftrack. The fighting, weather and the large distances involved in Russia meant that vehicles were in constant need of servicing or repair.

Waffen SS troops eat, relax and drink. The fierce fighting began to place a huge psychological strain on the troops, compounded by the fact that the failure of Operation Blue meant spare time away from the front was reduced.

Russian peasants with cattle joined by a yoke. For many poor people in Russian rural villages, life had changed little in the last 100 years. To the *Waffen SS* it merely confirmed Nazi propaganda that the Soviets were a primitive and backward people.

A *Waffen SS* soldier prepares for the next stage of the advance in an underground dugout. The German advance in 1942 was to come to a grinding halt at Stalingrad.

A *Waffen SS* band play an open air concert. Marching songs played a vital part in reinforcing the Nazi worldview and boosting morale. They were also popular with the troops as they reminded them of home.

Ambulances line up to take the wounded away, top, and a Fieseler Stork aircraft, bottom, prepares to take away a seriously wounded man. In 1942 medical supplies became increasingly difficult to transport due to the Soviet counter offensive and partisan activity. Consequently many were destined never to reach the front line.

A *Waffen SS* soldier checks the medical supplies. Away from the front line living conditions were extremely basic. Command posts also had to be packed up quickly in case of an attack by the Soviets.

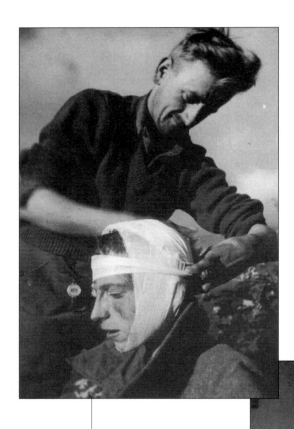

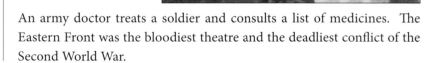

An army doctor treats a soldier and consults a list of medicines. The Eastern Front was the bloodiest theatre and the deadliest conflict of the Second World War.

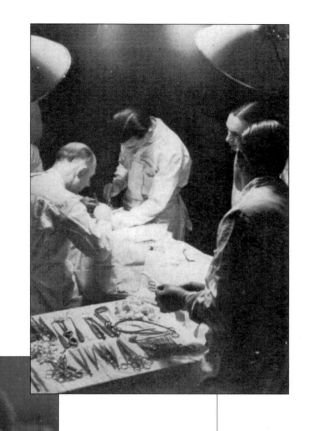

German propaganda showing a doctor treating a Soviet woman and surgeons operating on a civilian. In practice captured Soviet women and children were treated with exceptional brutality. Villages were massacred and civilian hostages routinely killed. By the end of the war over 20 million Russian citizens had been killed as a result of Operation Barbarossa.

The *Waffen SS* made extensive use of the *Volkswagen Type 166 Schwimmwagen* or swimming car. From 1941 to 1944 over 15,000 were made making it the most numerous mass produced amphibious car in history. For crossing the water a screw propeller was lowered down from the rear deck engine cover and a simple coupling connected it to the engine's crankshaft propelling the car forward. To go backwards in the water there was the choice of using a paddle or engaging reverse gear, allowing the turning wheels to slowly rotate the vehicle. The front wheels doubled up as rudders, so steering was done with the wheel on both land and water.

Reconnaissance attached to the *Waffen SS* played a vital part in the German advance and later the retreat from Russia, pinpointing enemy positions and searching for cover. Reconnaissance units were responsible for scouting ahead as SS Divisions were often in the vanguard of the fighting in Russia. The soldier, top, is using a scissors periscope.

A destroyed tank. In the three great battles of Moscow, Smolensk and Kiev in 1941 the Germans lost 7,000 tanks requiring then to reinforce the front with seventeen divisions from the West.

A Volkswagen *Kubelwagen* and a *10.5cm leFH 18 leichte FeldHaubitze* or light field howitzer move up to the front. The 10.5cm leFH 18 had a range of over 1000 metres and a fire rate of 4-6 rounds per minute.

Waffen SS troops watch the battle from their *Sonderkraftfahrzeug 251* or Sd.Kfz 251 armoured fighting vehicle built by the Hanomag company. Heavily armoured it was a versatile vehicle which was well liked by the troops and known simply as a *"Hanomag"* by both German and Allied soldiers.

A *Waffen SS* soldier tries to rescue his equipment from a flood. The torrential rains in the autumn of 1942 played havoc with the German advance. The Soviets were far better prepared and strategically used the Russian autumns and winters to their advantage, timing their attacks to coincide with lulls in the weather.

An infantry field gun is fired from underneath a camouflage net. Although nearly destroyed in 1941 the Soviet airforce became a much greater threat the following year. In April 1942, Lieutenant General Alexander Novikov took command and made it one unified force. Factories were also moved east of the Ural Mountains and began full production, contributing about 1000 planes a month.

Waffen SS troops get ready to attack. They were better equipped than the *Wehrmacht* and despite accounting for only a small proportion of the total number of German troops involved in the East, often lead the attack.

Waffen SS troops rescue a badly injured soldier. *Waffen SS Divisions* often received a far higher proportion of casualties than other army divisions reflecting their front line role and fanatical fighting.

Waffen SS Panzer tank commanders receive awards for bravery. *Sturmbannfuehrer* Christian Tyschen, middle, commander of the 2nd Company of the Panzer Regiman receives the Knights Cross. Walter Kuger, commander of *Das Reich*, bottom awards *Untersturmfuehrer* or section commander Karl-Heinz Boska with the German Cross in Gold. He later received the Knights Cross.

A soldier from the *8th SS Calvary Panzer Division Florian Geyer* holds an anti tank *"teller"* mine to use against a Russian T34 tank. Shaped like a plate and packed with 5.5 kilograms of high explosive with a detonation pressure of about 200 pounds, the teller mine was capable of blowing the tracks off any Soviet tank.

German heavy artillery moves up towards the front. The *17cm Kanone 18 Mörserlafette* or 17cm K 18 in MrsLaf was a heavy howitzer used extensively by the *Waffen SS*.

Although an excellent weapon the 17cm K 18 in MrsLaf was expensive to produce, difficult to manoeuvre and very slow to set up and take down. Many were lost when their crews destroyed them to avoid capture by advancing Soviet forces.

The 17cm K 18 in MrsLaf in action by day and night. It had a maximum range of 18 miles and was used to provide long range counter battery support.

A knocked out Panzer VI or Tiger tank in the rubble of Stalingrad. The Battle of Stalingrad marked the turning point in the East after which the Germans were on the defensive.

Waffen SS soldiers unload bicycles from a railway carriage in 1942. The German Army used several million bicycles during the Second World War but they were better suited to the good roads in Western Europe than the rough tracks in Russia.

An SS war correspondent records a report from the front line, July 1942. Censored reports appeared in the SS newspaper *Das Schwarze Korps* or the Black Corps edited by Gunter d'Alquen.

Heinrich Himmler inspecting *Waffen SS* troops, September 1942. He set up the SS Race and Resettlement Office to deliver Hitler's vision of *lebensraum* or living space for German people in the East. In it were plans to deport 14 million people from the steppes and forests of Russia to Siberia and replace them with over 2 million ethnic Germans.

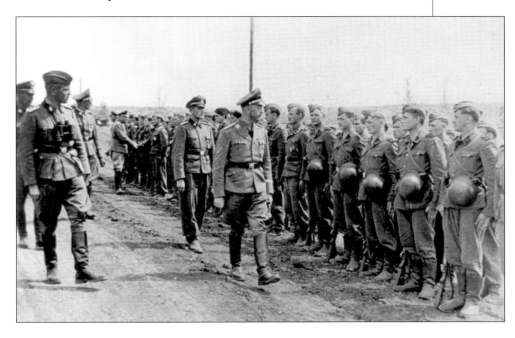

A parade of *Das Reich* troops saluting, 1942. The division was decimated following Army Group Centre failure to take Moscow and was sent to France to rest and regroup.

Obergruppenfuhrer Joseph Dietrich, centre, commander of the *Leibstandarte SS Adolf Hitler* poses with his officers in 1942. Dietrich ended the war as one of Nazi Germany's most decorated soldiers but was later tried for war crimes by both the Americans and Germans.

The *SS Wiking* division receiving Iron Crosses for bravery on the Eastern Front. The Iron Cross 2nd Class came with a black, white and red ribbon. In formal dress, the entire cross was worn mounted alone or as part of a medal bar but for everyday wear, only the ribbon was worn from the second button hole in the tunic.

A Panzer tank commences the German offensive to capture Stalingrad in the late summer of 1942. By the end of the year the German campaign in the East had come to a halt. The Battle of Stalingrad was the largest battle on the Eastern Front and was a crushing defeat for Germany. It was a turning point in the war and after it the German forces never again had a major strategic victory in the East.

More from the same series

Most books from the 'Eastern Front from Primary Sources' series are edited and endorsed by Emmy Award winning film maker and military historian Bob Carruthers, producer of Discovery Channel's Line of Fire and Weapons of War and BBC's Both Sides of the Line. Long experience and strong editorial control gives the military history enthusiast the ability to buy with confidence.

The series advisor is David McWhinnie, producer of the acclaimed Battlefield series for Discovery Channel. David and Bob have co-produced books and films with a wide variety of the UK's leading historians including Professor John Erickson and Dr David Chandler. Where possible the books draw on rare primary sources to give the military enthusiast new insights into a fascinating subject.

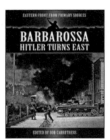
Barbarossa

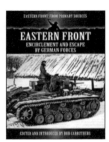
Eastern Front: Encirclement

Götterdämmerung

Eastern Front: Night Combat

The Waffen SS in the East 1941-1943

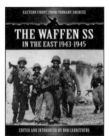
The Waffen SS in the East 1943-1945

The Wehrmacht Experience in Russia

Winter Warfare

The Red Army in Combat

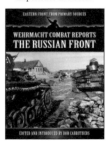
Wehrmacht Combat Reports: The Russian Front

For more information visit www.pen-and-sword.co.uk